T0273703

CAILLEACH

Leanne O'Sullivan was born in 1983, and comes from the Beara peninsula in West Cork. She received an MA in English from University College, Cork in 2006. The winner of several of Ireland's poetry competitions, including the Seacat, Davoren Hanna and RTE Rattlebag Poetry Slam, she has published two collections, both from Bloodaxe, *Waiting for My Clothes* (2004) and *Cailleach: The Hag of Beara* (2009), winner of the Rooney Prize for Irish Literature in 2010, with a third collection, *The Mining Road*, due out in 2013.

Her work has been included in various anthologies, including Selina Guinness's *The New Irish Poets* (Bloodaxe Books, 2004) and Billy Collins' *Poetry 180: A Turning Back to Poetry* (Random House, 2003). Residencies and festival readings have taken her to France, India and China, among other places and she was the recipient of the 2009 Ireland Chair of Poetry bursary.

LEANNE O'SULLIVAN

CAILLEACH

THE HAG OF BEARA

BLOODAXE BOOKS

ISBN: 978 1 85224 818 5

First published 2009 by
Bloodaxe Books Ltd,
Eastburn,
South Park,
Hexham,
Northumberland NE46 1BSP.

www.bloodaxebooks.com
For further information about Bloodaxe titles
please visit our website and join our mailing list
or write to the above address for a catalogue.

Supported using public funding by
**ARTS COUNCIL
ENGLAND**

Cover design: Neil Astley & Pamela Robertson-Pearce.

Ditital reprint of the 2009 Bloodaxe Books edition.

For Andrew,
my love.

ACKNOWLEDGEMENTS

Acknowledgements are due to the editors of the following publications in which some of these poems first appeared: *Agenda*, *Cork Literary Review*, *Best of Irish Poetry 2008*, edited by Thomas McCarthy & Bríd Ní Mhóráin (Southword Editions, 2007), *Best of Irish Poetry 2008*, edited by Paul Perry & Nuala Ní Chonchúir (Southword Editions, 2008), *The March Hare Anthology*, edited by Adrian Fowler (Breakwater Press, 2006), *Poetry Ireland Review*, *The Shop*, *Southword*, *The Stinging Fly*, *The Stony Thursday Book*, ed. Thomas McCarthy (2008), *World Literature Today* and www.poetryinternational.org.

I am also grateful to An Chomhairle Ealaíonn/The Arts Council for a generous bursary in 2007. I would like to thank Professor Gearóid Ó Crualaoich for his kind reading of the poems and his study, *The Book of the Cailleach: Stories of the Wise-Woman Healer* (Cork University Press, 2003).

It's also a pleasure to acknowledge the help and support of: Pat Cotter and the Munster Literature Centre; Steve, Caron and Ilona at the Arvon Foundation, Lumb Bank; and Sue Booth-Forbes at Anam Cara.

CONTENTS

IV THE UNKNOWABLE PLACE

V STONE

OPPOSITE: *An Cailleach Bhéarra / The Hag of Beara, Ballycrovane Harbour, Beara Peninsula (photo: Donal O'Sullivan)*

CAILLEACH

I

Path

I will begin again with the stories, though I fear I am drawing out a thing unfinished, moving still in half-light. My pleasures I remember, the ones that remained and enfold me, like my unborn in shoals of light, the unwearied smiles of those dreams. I raise the haunting things, shadowed impresses of the earth. They are the resin of people I once touched, lingering between my vision now and my vision then. But I must resist the old distractions. Age continues with its backward glances, with all its ghosts, and one layer of stone settles on another.

Birth

Now comes November,
my birth time, and white ribs of tide
uproot the silence of the bay.

Today I break from stone onto sand,
motherless, my mother a stone
bedding the earth and dreaming my image.

I stretch like a snail from a deep sleep,
my flesh gathering its warm fabrics
and unknitting me from this womb.

I listen and mimic the flood-tide,
open my ears to the haul of shells,
sheer salts erupting my birth-cry.

My eyes lift as the day begins
to shape itself, light being emptied
into it as a soft fall of rain sweeps

my moss-lined palms. I tread
into this soaked brightness,
bogland and the air full of fuchsia.

This is the blood and bone of my mother,
sheets of grass and weed – all her flushing skins
I lean on with my hands and knees.

Feeling a thirst gently pull
I bring my mouth to the fall of water
from a leaf to taste the cool, plentiful drops.

I shake the drench from branches, my limbs
and lips moving fluently, the way a full throat
learns to move for its earliest swallowing.

Scent

I have touched these chambers before,
my body says, when I lie on the bed of a king,
watching his indigo riches strip to the floor.
His heart flutters like a moth against glass,
or those dancers coupled along the halls of his castle.

He's never sure what to hold or whisper,
my body inching like a fox, breasts swaying
like two pale moons over his quilted bed
where I've often left flowers – daisies, dandelions,
and honeysuckle for his pillow, the threads
of which still show the hollow made of his cheek.

Still it is night outside, still his jewelled hand
on my back while I unfasten my hair in the hour
when everything is sheeted down with darkness.
I lay my fingers to the fever on his chest
and curl my prints there, ridge and glen.

His scent like burning flesh softens into my skin.
I crawl to him, calm fierceness, over the pillows
and roses, flags of blood marking my tread
across his legs where I kiss and break open,
until he starts to moan, grass-sweet drippings
of his mouth, as though he's making me a gift
in the quiet before each breath, guiding my tongue
back along the path none but another animal could follow.

Sister

It wasn't my calf she killed that screamed its absence
but the green viciousness in her eye, exploding
like water over coals as she tasted the blood.
No sooner she slaughtered than she ran, smiling, and I after her
up the soft slopes, my skirts chiming against the grass.
Sister bitch. She was always a cocky thing, but slow.

Honestly, I preferred her dead, her black teeth
chilling in the mud like an afterbirth.
So we planned a war for morning, after breakfast.
When the houses began to yawn their shadows
I dressed warmly, climbed the mountain and piled rocks
by my ankles – size, weight and number, a stone for her side.

Hissing, she stood on an opposite hill flinging her stones,
missing me one by one. The sun couldn't throw such fires.
I hit back at her cat-calls, her blood, her startled face
as her slim feet began to stumble on the ledge.
Every rock I threw tunnelled through the air
and drowned her ears with their dullness.

I charmed her tongue to such sweetness then.
She cried reason, so I reasoned with that, seeing her look down
where the grey rocks open like the rageless mouths of rooks.
I admit she held her fists until the end, her arms spinning
and spinning in the wind's loom. Just as she staggered
to the edge I readied my smile and flung my last – a breath,
a clear breath sister, to help when your balance snaps.

The Stones Turning into Mountains

Like shadows courted
between the rushes
they climb, one by one,

in the night-ebb
over the borders
of the rain-waxed fields,

dropping their lichen loads,
their fossil-robes,
their darkly pitched breaths.

Their upward crumbling
is an almost sparkling stream,
burying the bright stars

in the belly of their cave,
while the smaller ones
rattle, shouldering aside

the opened soil,
and ferry their echoes
in the earth's swelling.

Between clay sockets
and clustered vetchling
the eyes squat baldly,

nourishing the rills
of spring-water,
the copper pleating.

It is easy to perish
so entirely
in the hard dark.

In a year they will stand
perfectly in the cold
corner of the eye.

The mountain
with its rings of stone,
its whole body unfolded

arches itself out
like a shadow among
the lakebeds.

The heather ascended,
they root their stare, their tongues
prickling with light.

About Midnight

Among these wet, berry skins
I sit with my back to the wall,

cross-legged, smiling my red mouth.
I've settled myself into a soft corner,

my eyes moving quickly, circling
the high, loud limbs of the night.

In the centre of the dance floor
a lioness screams in her own bath.

Like red pearls, dry lips pucker
to the eager glass. I drink and blaze.

An animal going mad for the garland
of a woman rolls over to the end

of the bar like a devil's tongue, red
and greasy, sweet in his own poison

and licking his lips. A man in love
spreads a flock of fingers on my thigh.

I undo them until he hates me
and raise an eye to his back.

The room is flooding, people float
as if on a singing ocean. I stumble

onto my feet and drown in the night-smells,
while the moon turns onto her white belly

and is fed secrets by crippled mouths;
the music carried through the walls,

a glass shattered, a woman tasted
with her legs wrapped around a man,

the night moistening the darkness
with its many breaths.

Autumn

The stars vanished during the night, in the stillness,
and the sun lifted like a pale hand over the hush.
Afterwards, I lay beneath a blanket my mother wove.
My arms felt her mouth sigh; I breathed in the earth,
feeling my way along the paths and hatching light.

This morning the pine trees sap the damp air,
sunshine and moonshine are misted together
with closeness, shivering a musk of dew from the grasses.

Gold morning, and the ocean rises over the rocks.
I learn to count in suns, to hear the morning
as if I were pressing my ear to its moist pulse.
I learn to smell the hoops of bramble berry in the dark.

The Watcher and the First Sight

Between the water-sharded stones
and the whispering banks
I knelt watching you, my body
like a dark sun over the groping roots.
I knew the river by its hug of marsh,
the myriad eyes of frog spawn
floating softly in their soaked nests.

I knelt there, watching you,
your legs and waist disappearing
in the stream as though you were half woven
from water, lifting your nets like a creature
with its scales when the sun comes sifting down.
I have never so much trespassed, I thought,
as you bent into the crushing water,
the taut coolness of your skin
shining with the crystal salt.

I did not want a glance or a sound,
only the sight of you – the mouthing space,
the absence of language; only to watch you
turn through the shimmering coils of light,
the river rising around me, describing to me
the dark that would be cast over the body,
violent, liquid, salt, calm –
the darkness that would be cast
between the moment when I could destroy
and the moment when I would devour.

II

The Unwhispered Hush

I am drowning in your dark-cast mouthings. My lips won't join. My hair falls like soaked feathers against my back; my legs are collapsed and glinting silver, like mackerel tails in moonlight. Water descends the walls of my house, and blooms the smell of stone, pouring out anything calm. We are both trembling on the floor. I touch out words with my tongue – I adore your body, I adore your mouth – but what remains when these things quiver? Is there no safe and knowable place? All those gems you have set your heart to – your nets, your songs, your skin – all will shatter if you stir.

River

You were the first thought the world had
when it dipped its palms and made rivers,
the grass banks sweetened and sealed
with dew, wells of healing, uneven
chanting of stones, let be, let come.

Your birth stepping quietly into light,
light wiping back the declining night.
I knew you then, restful, unknowing,
ebony in the fleshing sea, love humming
a syllable I would know you by.

Turn again. Show me your sweetness.
Bending my face to the river's lap
I can feel you, clearly, reaching up,
braiding my hair, speaking my name,
everything suddenly, beautifully, touchable.

Offering

In the late afternoon I look up from my work
and see you standing at my gate, hand paused
on the rusty bolt like a gannet waiting to plunge.
Under your arm you balance a box of fish,
radiant mackerel, the shocked stare of pollock.

The smell of fish is fading like a scar silvering
on your skin, and you step towards me,
let the box down gently onto the grass.
My eyes and ears follow your footfall
across the path where you come to sit beside me.

I hold a gaze to the plentiful tails curved
and leaning out of the box, the pure cry,
the throwing off of flesh, and the scent of you
I take in, the long and calm breath gathered
for the sweetness after the feast is done.

The Bridge

I want to stay with you tonight, as light unhusks
and spills slowly from the half-moon,
where I am lying curved beside you in the dark.

I know you by touch, our bodies finding the other,
kiss by kiss, like birds flying in pattern,
breast to breast and legs intertwined.

Your flesh glitters, shadowless, round droplets
rising in dew. I cannot be near enough.
I remember the first night our skins were this close,

after a day of rain, a bridge shining behind you
in the blind wilderness. I heard the crunch
of leaves under my feet, the small distance

of a bird's cry as I moved closer to you,
one half of a creature guided out of the dark,
trails of goose-pimples along my skin.

Months later I think of it, leaning against you,
as if on the lip of a boat, and the clouds
unloosing their nets until the full rain came again,

moving everything in one direction, tremendous as a cell
and brushing against the whole nerve of my body,
in the dew hours, your lips on my forehead.

Promise

The grey sound of rain on the roof,
sound and light splitting on my skin
like flint pieces working me; I am preparing
a place for you, cleaning down the walls
and worktops, making space in the wide rooms,
in the small rooms, doubling things needed.
Roses I found growing around the bridge
I lay on your pillow; though time and love
go round like dancers, in time I won't be able
to tell your name from mine, to separate
your voice from my voice within this house.
My love I am at the table, waiting.
When you come home my hands shake
like rain breaking on the knotted waves.

Sleep Love

Still dark, you leave early, the night
a quiet blue shuddering and I sleep
alone into the dawn, my shoulders
and hip-bones fitting the bed's grooves,
the sheet curved to my knees and folded
where you were last calm beside me,
like a soft water floating on all sides,
gentle sills of your sleeping weight
filling the length of the bed.

I curve to the absence of your curve,
hold to your learnt shape, touch, rest.
I stretch towards the clasping of your scent
on the pillow, the tiny rain mist of breath
coming out to me, morning-fisted at dawn,
then easing out calmly as if through your spirit
when you sleep, heaven conscious and warm.

For an hour I love to want you,
knowing merciless love, the visible silk of it,
the touchable paths, and each morning-crest
sliding me over our pillow nest,
your scent like a shy prayer I burrow into,
the unwhispered hush of your sleep I sleep to.

The Meeting Place

The mist rolls from the hills like an airy moss,
mottled with heather, and my weather-eye
is cast to the clouds hanging wildly above us.

On the strand you have pulled like a cage
the pitch of your legs around mine to hold me,
until we seem almost knotted to a doubled self.

This is the sea at the end of it;
the sky and the sea's tangled cries flooding
inwards, then out to the grey reflection of itself.

I am lost in this encircling.
Your head behind mine comes to rest
in the crook of my shoulder,

and you say 'look' again and again
so that the coming rain has some order
about it, walking with gestures and signals.

I lift your hand into mine and press down
on it with my mouth. In this water-scape
one of us has entered the other,

so that there is only touch and the uplift of breath
to see you by. Like a map your body comes to me,
breasted to the storm-hauled waves. I tell you,

I would follow you into the rain-thorned water,
harnessed by your limbs, if only for you
to see the calmness of my eyes now.

Whirlpool

'Down there,' he said, and I looked down
along the sheer cliff drop to the ocean.
'Down there at the bottom is a whirlpool
and takes everything to another place.'

I picked up a rock and dropped it in,
porous and dark. It soared down
like something courageous, as though
it was committing its first and only act.

Then, in the stillness before it disappeared,
hour of timeless motion, hour of cold workings,
I felt its weight push down to release itself,
the angle of the cliff's edge slightly swaying
as if the earth was unfolding like a scroll.

Down there, he said, and I looked down.
My God, my terrors, my fantastic,
I tell you, there it happens; ocean, salt, sky,
a tent of words, eyes open, each wave
sweeping out like bursting glass.

III

The Purple Wave

And there was a well below the sea, and the nine hazels of wisdom grew there. Their leaves and blossoms broke within the same hour and fell in a shower that raised a purple wave. And the five salmon that were waiting there ate the nuts so that their scales glowed brighter with their magic. They swam to the seven rivers of wisdom that sprung up from the well. If someone were to eat one of those salmon, they would devour all the knowledge of the world. That was the story, how it was told, in the hundred fire-lit homes, the smuggling in of myth.

Storyteller

(for Michelle Power)

Late evening, a woman carries back to her home
turf marked with the dark green stalkings
of the field, the brown nakedness of the hills.

The cattle move sleepily in their stone shed,
their milk-warm scent woven into her clothes.
People are getting ready, tapping out hours

and the weave of the backroads
until the hedged outlines rise
like phantoms against the dark.

On the top of a hill they make out
a light between the alders,
a small torch risen out of the earth.

And the woman bends over her fire,
hands stretched open, nettle-sting withdrawing
on her arms as she scatters

the shattered pieces of turf over the flames,
wind scorched, shrug of the spade,
whispering, *my words, my words,*

as their bodies reach soothingly out of the blaze.

Hazel

I saw the tree growing inside me,
up from my ankles, circling my waist,
brimming my earthed belly.

Its whole beauty flowered in my skin,
came trembling like sea creatures
blown from the ocean.

Why was I given this skin, this blood,
warm and human, until the wind blows
and I feel a whorl of leaves on my tongue?

The sunlight falls like gold and white silk
through the giant bones and eyes.
I shake the pollen from my hair

and hear the crows cry in the embrace
of branches. They are turning their mouths up,
call by call. The darkness too is there.

I am waist-deep in it, pulling myself
up from the ground, the thirsting earth,
rising from it with my green feast.

Big House

Now they are gathering in the field –
that's my neighbour standing
shawled amongst them, dressed in black
and facing the heavy frame of a doorway.

Last week I stood waist-deep in the water
and watched the villagers take pieces of drift
from the strand, their palms and elbows
full of stones that shone like newborn faces.

They were building this, large house
and a dark door facing the ocean.

*

The sky passes over like a grey animal
and in the distance I can smell the rain coming.
I wonder do they notice, or do they feel the cold.

They are opening the doors now and begin to flow,
one long line, into its stomach. I follow,
a soundless shell, moved by something I can't name.

They are solemn and clasping their hands,
wrapped up in themselves like sleeping birds.

The chill settles on my throat. I am a stranger here,
a mind barren among these others.

My eyes are moving like a baby's hand among
the salt hardened stones, the mouth-flame of candles.

There's the man that lead us in; gliding up
the middle passage, bodiless under all those robes,
with crests of gold embroidery rising with his lungs.

His breath flickers on the candles, stretching their light
to every corner, and for a moment there is a gathering of eyes.

*

When I leave I will take this with me – death and life
sweating in the stones, and that untouchable light.

I am alone with these breathing heads, staring at the stones,
the moist spots of ocean I touched before.

I remember the lightening white of waves,
that fragrant moan I slept with as a child,

letting my head sway in its lap, and breathe in
what I breathed there once.

*

The room makes one deep sound
like curraghs swaying together.

The man at the table is speaking – he speaks
but the ocean comes to my ears.

When the people kneel,
I kneel with them, trembling.

When they sing I bow my head,
unhook the spade of my tongue
and mouth my silences.

Children of the Cillínach

Come to us with lilies and meadowsweet,
come to us by heart and not by sight,
that heaving of love which aches still,
coffined in your belly's darkening loam.

Mother, I've known your weight
and the length of your soft hands
bent over this rugged, unworked soil.
I've known you by the forgetful daisies

strung with blue and red twine.
I open my eyes; you are watching me.
If ever I am allowed a voice
you will know me when I speak:

if I were unwinged in nothingness I would
bring home to you a memory of wings.
The scythe which undercuts life I remember,
and above, a chorus of birds, the petals

of daisies lifting. Hear me;
I will know you again among the crickets
and billowing trees. We will survive the earth.
Are you not my mother?

Was it not you I heard in the thrashing dark?
The one whose hands
I felt unbury me and baptise my soul
in a fountaining of tears?

Rumour

Once I was rumoured to have killed a man,
a lover of mine, to forget money he stole.
The voices rolled to a greedy mass down the village,
disturbing my faults. I wore black, I bowed.
I learned to speak with looks instead of words.

Nevertheless, I wasn't fearful; I felt his absence,
tight like a bandage around my mouth,
and wore it out. Even now I think of him,
pick of the bunch, my pucker-faced eel.
He kept coming to my gate, looking at me

with a feverish pallor. It was his hands
that wooed me, those bootsole palms
large and warm, clambering around my waist.
But what of his eyes, close as hairs,
grooved above his full white cheeks?

Or his lips? Those two hot wires that entered
my mouth, sliding shut sometimes
on a secret. Such sweetheart shrieks I remember,
and what I missed – his infinite jaw,
his glassy teeth bleeding their light, his smile.

The rumours didn't end, became gestures,
like branches nodding. I walked the village
wearing my new clothes, quietly,
my arms swinging.

Little One, My Mother Said

Never were you a child with me
the way children are children
with mothers, pulp of their skin,
small love on their arm, but so near
that I couldn't be sure whose heart
I crossed when I wished you here,
fleshed and doubled my flesh,
fired and exploded my fire.

Your red hair pulsed upward
amongst the gull-grey stones.
O, my little one, I am speaking now
with your accent, spring furled
on my tongue like a pearl. The land
is a map with my palm-lines,
the stars and moonbeams flow
over the pouts of my cheek.

You see the hung fuchsia deepening
again the touch of love –
            by which I have
more than your touch, but life flown
out of my skin like a dream –
my love-line to your life-line,
and the blazing hours of light
bending slowly over you.

Lost

Having watched the flashing shoals all day
he went out in the late evening with the men.
The mackerel and nets and the distant houses
seemed to be made from silver or a grey steel
under the moonless shroud of dark over the bay.
I watched the silhouette of my love's head
set like a heart in the follower boat, his back bent
as if he would heave them all out alone from the pier.

I felt it before I heard it, pressed it to my skin,
my lips, eyes, my palms. It became as visible
as the lighthouse light icing through the shadows.
An hour before his boat went down I ran my hand
over his small bedside cupboard, followed the stream
of his mornings around the room. It was as if the shell
of his breathing that drew a shape in his pillow
suddenly weakened, fell slack as a cheek in that nest.

When the morning rose I waited
behind the kitchen window, watching the sea lull quiet.
I thought of a blinding dawn, and the world underneath.
I thought of the foxgloves waiting in the meadows.
I felt it before they told me, the cold, the tuneless shriek.
Up from the darkened landings the last few came,
bearing their knives and lure, their hands pickled,
bright as fish, rising slowly in the ebb tide.

IV

The Unknowable Place

The ocean became the beating thing within me; the landscape, the animals, the skies, the sloping waves of soil became my garments, and I walked shrouded in my old elements, without companion. Nothing echoed my voice, my footsteps. I had lost a skin – that curved, murmuring otherness that returns a voice. I went to the shore, the air around it filled with a white mist of hovering light. I did not weep. I sat on a sponge of grassless earth, watched the light rise to its brightest peak and sink again, and I breathed in – darkest heather, the peaceable clay, the ochre dawn. Astounded by sorrow, all night I sat and listened to my breath.

Rapture

I dreamed that when I turned from the strand
I saw a furze bush shivering up on the hill.
And the bush itself a moving calm;
when I crawled beneath it I found your hands,
trembling together, dusted gold with the fallen petals.

I gathered them into my arms and kissed them,
kissed away the bloom of mud from your palms,
kissed and kissed wildly the needle wounds,
the grooves of your knuckle buds, their cold light
spreading like a scent in the lightening-blistered twilight.

Back on the shore I found your chest,
dashed with shingle and knuckled with cold.
All together I found your arms, feet, ribs, your face
glistening like a jewelled heart among the limpets,
and the gift of your lips brought to my face like a cloth.

When I had pieced you together you were still,
and I lay with you, pressed the soft clay of my flesh
into your hollows, as if we were not separate.
I did not move. Like a barnacle to your side, Love,
until the tide turns its coats, and the world unfastens me.

The Waiting

An image of flame cresting like waves
on the horizon line, the sun goes down
to drink its own widening light –
light, pink as an eggshell, slips calmly
along the waves, the curling out of night.
Water has shattered the light
and the tiny fragments play in my hands.
My eyes hold to this beautiful shred
and the stones revolve in the tide.
Nothing but the sea, its light-rimmed breath,
draws the cold out of me like a bone.

Search Boats

Already signals are beginning to return the boats.
Searchlights are scattering on the waves
like an old room filled with a dust caught sparkling
on the pouring-in of sunlight. One by one the boats
come back, retrieving their exhausted shadows.
Big-shouldered and small-shouldered men
stand around me like one upright nerve
nodding and dropping their silenced faces.

The two fraying sheets of my lips closed together,
immeasurable breath held beneath my lungs,
so no one heard; I remember when I brought
my summer stung lips to yours and felt
the gentle moorings of your mouth,
its moistness rippling against mine,
as if you were swallowing, clasping,
humming without language or sound –

It was just shy of being tender, as though touch
skulked like an animal beneath your breath.
I saw so closely the honey-green skin of your eyes
that it seemed we were becoming one entire creature,
buoyant and shuddering. Now, at the end of our joining,
I look down to the hollowing waves. I am speared to this pier,
as if fastened beside you, my mouth wrapped
in your breath-beat, and the crumbling places
of love where we became so utterly one.

The Dancing Rooms

Then they called 'Melodeon Jim' to play,
and I heard through the sets of dancers
his gathering the chord notes in the box,
a riddled mounting to the tune-path.

The sound strikes against the frame
of the room and you take my hand gently
into the gleaming middle of the music,
the cross-stitch of movements in lamplight.

All night the bay foams in the rock pools
like a thousand fallen swan feathers,
secretly as young girls arranging their hair,
something seen in the backward glances.

Our feet and bodies batter on the boards,
an enunciation of language on skin,
more breathless and luminous than the currents
of words lost upon the tongue.

Those who came from the island bring
the taste of salt and shingle on their lips,
and hear the music as a net cast out.
You and I hear it as a mirror hung

over the sea, the petals of light falling
on the crest of each small wave,
falling everywhere and everywhere lost.
The names of moths come clear to me now –

Swallowtail, True Lover's-Knot, White Ermine
marbled against the lamplight. When we first
danced together you were poised perfectly,
turning the steps and half said words

into my body's rhythms, the quiet of things done.
Again I follow you into your summer moods,
holding the last echo of a beat within a beat.
Here is my hand held out. Give me another.

When You Died

When you died I burrowed your name
into an oak's crippling bark with my fingernails,
curled it between the ribbed grooves,
reading with my eyes love and lover,
a touch I carry withering in my breast.
I returned to know the dark, to remember
and name your warm, work-rough skin
that held a shelter above me,
made the earth soft and salt-scented.

I did not notice the years' slow embering
and I scatter what's left, the flaking wood,
bald roots flickering above the mud
and how it felt to sleep with your palms
drawn across my back, sated and breakable,
curl of your elbow cradling my neck.

Little blisterings, like headstones, rise from the bark
as I trace a small wholeness of you,
a name I whisper, and polish between my lips.
I leave you there with the heartless shadows,
the oak-casket of your death, the dark scars
your love has left its touch upon.

Swimming Lessons

Morning, the touching of the moon
on the oval-line of light, the sun low,
its fire like liquid over the ocean
where the wading gulls hunt. I toed
the foam and smooth sand as a rattle of salt
rushed against my skin, the pebbles,
the water's joyful touchings.

I waded up to my chin,
let my head cradle into the palm of a wave,
its tongue wiping me down, filling me
and pulling me in while my hair pulsed
outwards like a shredded skin.

If I went under I could see
what the waves cling to – stone,
the haul of weed, the strong thrash at once
heat and ice, sound and soundlessness
yawning up, cloud-shadows dragging
on the sea-bed like melting iron.

The water gloved my body,
changed my skin and the white season
of my face, cup around the crown of my head,
palm to my body like an unhurried gift.
I saw the ribbon-length of waves
sinking my clothes into the sand,
as if two worlds were touching in moans,
trembling the air, the glowing fog,
the muffled globe of the moon
sliding my legs quietly into the sea.

Her Husband Says

At the end of my life
there was the twilight pleated

between the clouds,
and the memory of that evening

I brought safely with me –
when the sun, gold and silent,

slid from the sky and beneath
our room, I stood beside you,

watching the rain at the window
your hands cupped to my chest.

Outside, the noiselessness of winter,
the moon fleshing over the village,

and the leaves gathering
on the roadside.

I looked at you, against the pane,
still and glistening

as if I saw you through the whole
of my life, our moist breaths

shrouding our faces together
in the dark bending of the earth.

I said that the leaves will come,
deep green shadows

rising over the frost after I am gone.
I told you that you would stand here again

after the first winter. You would
call for me, and in my absence know

how the quiet after grief comes
slowly, like the quiet after love.

V

Stone

And I have misremembered; things shuffled off the shelves, things settled or bargained for. Yet there are minutes when the lighted sod of memory is passed, and I feel myself dissolved in time, so that the years rise and set, and I hear them only as the tide turning in the distance. Layer upon layer, the stone clasps around me, and my eyes fall to where the sea and mountains meet. Old desires sound on my skin like flames breaking in the woods. Yes. Everything is done.

Birth Dream

Once I made mountains, carried stones and earth
in my apron and set them in piles along the coast,
raised them up like the skin of a healing wound.
They are old now, and I am still here, wading
the river's clay bed to the lush meadow on the east.

My daughter moves in me. All night I dreamed
her breath coming through my belly and wondered
if she could smell the grass, its startled dew floating
over the smallness of her, or if she could grasp
in her soft quarry the green light flushing my skin.

I follow the worn sheep path to the hill-top
and look out to the blue and grey ocean,
the shadows of doorways, the stubble of red fields.
My hands lift into the falling husks of light.
They pool in my eyes, and drop from me like a scent.

I remember a world that was then only earth and stone,
I remember my love rising from the water, green and golden
in sunlight, ferrying back in his arms the glowing weed.
Now, I am taking back my first shape, aged and round
as when I lay shadowed in the heart of a stone.

I am making plans. I have planted and made harvest,
I have raked the soil and brought back clods
of sweet and fragrant earth. I lay in an intimacy of love
that came like a dream of this child, moistening my body
so that she could slide safely into it.

The sun is coming now. My child bunches her little fist.
In the dawn our shadow lies down onto the grass,
and the sea explodes below us. I am beginning another miracle,
rising here before the dew, the root, the bloom,
drawing from stone my daughter's precious and tiny face.

How Old

When my visitor asked me how old I was
I told him to count one year for each bald bone
of a bullock he found in my house.

Pressing a curse into the air he hauled himself
up to the attic and began tossing, counting bones
into the downstairs room, murmuring beneath

the clatter, the rattle, the brittle echo
the shocked toss the heave the pitch
the cast and catch the cracking hurl –

He'd been told I was a witch,
my house a den of blood
slurred with the salty stench of flesh.

He looked for marks, for rings, for bloodied limbs.
For a day and a night and a day I stayed
in the downstairs room sniffing and loving his doubts,
his disgust, and the pile of old fevers, death-white now.

When I first heard them,
my thousand thousand memories falling around me,
I felt a flush, like a birth pain,
as if my body echoed what it heard,
remembering my pleasures, my hungers.

I turn in the early dark to remember –
one night in this room the small ecstasies,
fierce, shuddering, solder of the skin
the flame when, later, I asked for more.

I am filled with it, almost savouring his anger,
hands shredded to the wrist, an armful of answers,
guesses, squinted eyes, thumbing the numbers
against his fingertips.

And down he comes with a bone for a tongue,
rattling out his reasons and loathing,
his neighbourly stories and boastings.

I noticed his hands shake as he went for the door,
the fear in the deep couch of his face as he swore.

I drove him out with numbers,
the years within my mind,

one of the anguish and adoring parts,
one with a scent, the love notes high in my throat,
one of a stone cradle gleaming with dew,

the haunting things – when I was a woman
lying on my back by the whispering lakeside
and the ground around me was strewn with flowers.

The Saint's Sleep

He went down in a heavy summer heat
under the melodic weight of the sun,
a sea-tang glittering, a book beneath
his head as he lay on the cnocáin.

'Master, Master,' the voices called,
and he crawled farther down, down
to a husky sleep, faster towards
the rapture-grounds. 'Master, Master,'

the voices called, chanting their fierce
and various love, cleansing sorrows
at his feet, this in them and that in me,
cold green blades bending low.

He crouched in the soft dust of a dream;
in the church voices were closing doors,
hands were arranging pots of flowers.
Still, in this darkness, their eyes,

their faces appear as glowing stars,
and look down to him, slowly and cold.
'Master, Master,' the voices called
as he slipped farther, farther down.

The Wanderer

Would you walk with me, woman?
The cold is in for the night now,
and the mountains quiet. It's scarce
the sun rolls around her face
or walks out in the fields. The cold is in.
Would you walk with me, woman?

The night makes a blaze of my grief,
my only soft and finest love.
Her long hair is flung out before me
like moonlight on the sea.
All the memory of her is me.
Would you walk with me, woman?

I have no talk of war or song,
I have no ready ear to the earth
or words in passion for their work.
Sooner comes the dark engrained
on summits, and the ocean louder.
Would you walk with me, woman?

One more road in a whirl of roads
opens before me like a ritual of place.
I remember the foreign lightness of her touch.
I loved her soft and undecipherable notes.
The mountains are dark now. The cold is in.
Would you walk with me, woman?

Crow

I am calling you out, my first companion.
My eye to your eye sees only the fluid-dark,
the landscape of your iris brilliant as a rose.

I looked in, found two eyes, a face like my own
gathering its stone nets, the body forgetting
the body, the voice driven finally out to the earth.

Though it was only a nest of rags and one constant eye
that raised you I cherished a likeness there,
an unmoved beauty, so that when the time came

you would stand by the gentle lake sipping and foraging.
Your eyes would suddenly lighten with the swaying water,
calm and useful, they would look down and know me.

Dawn

I have only woken for one.
To the history that gave

me my name, I close my eyes.
All moons in me breathe

the dew of his breath.
It is a world of light now,

my heart to his mouth,
his hand to my heart.

I sing before these altars,
a psalm from the living vein

of heart and thought,
of dawn and season.

I become a ballad of light,
resonating with those prayers.

I am unfolded and unfolding,
rising slowly to the morning.

Never did my mouth
move like this.

When I close my eyes to kiss him
he is the centre –

my only sight of touch
and sound –

delicious shadows,
mouthfuls of light,

a breath held deeply
ending the end of my life.

The Return

I walk through paw-prints
the frost has dug,
among the moist grasses,
my silver hair flowing
like a cat's deep stretch.

This is my season.
Again and again I die
under the blossom of leaves
and count my lives
by the sapped rings of trees.

No one will know me,
none but the wood growth,
its hug of frost
its scent of moss
its naked shadow

and I, standing at the end
of an embered wood
where once a light
passed through me
and passes again,

before I remember
how I appeared
or how I ended,
folding myself into my arms –

the seed,
the root,
the blossom,
the stone shining
with all my running juices.